Howard Zinn
Just War

HOWARD ZINN
JUST WAR

FOREWORD BY GINO STRADA

PHOTOGRAPHS BY MOISES SAMAN

CHARTA

Foreword

Gino Strada

The Abolition of War:
A Reasonable Utopia Against an Unreasonable
Realism

During a talk in Rome on June 23, 2005, Howard Zinn
recalled a dramatic personal experience to express his
firm belief that "a just war" does not exist.
He volunteered in the American Army Air Force
against Nazism, bombing a French village that, seen
from above, was merely a target on a map. He visited
the village many years after the war ended, and he
immediately realized that war is in the first place
killing, death, destruction.
From that moment onward, he understood that the
victims on the ground, not the actions taking place in
the sky, are the only reality of war.
He accepted EMERGENCY's invitation to come to
Rome because he shared with us the idea that war can
be understood only through the experiences of the
victims. For this reason it is something unthinkable
that cannot be justified for any reason or any end. Not
even if a "good cause" is sincerely proclaimed: human
rights, justice, freedom, democracy.

Turning to war means, in fact, denying the very essence of these objectives.

War, some say, "has always existed." It's true, but the same thing can be said of many crimes, without a never-ending loop transforming these into condonable actions. Why in the world should repetition be a justification? Can't it, on the contrary, affirm the necessity of a new and more determined refusal?

The fact that war belongs to the past does not mean that it has to be part of the future as well. What would we think about this criterion if applied to diseases that in the past were incurable, but which today can be treated and oftentimes prevented?

Only a dull minded may consider impossible what has not happened yet.

People used to believe that only Newton's physics exists, until Albert Einstein had the courage (or naïvete) to ask himself "What if . . ." What followed was a new era in the history of physics, of science and culture.

It was not sheer indignation or faint desire, but a new culture that led Einstein himself to say: "War cannot be humanized, it can only be abolished!"

The intention to "humanize" war has led to the so-called

humanitarian law: a collection of rules that were
supposed to regulate the treatment of civilians and
prisoners of war. An honest analysis of the facts leads us
to realize that these rules have never placed a limit on
the behavior of either side. Their effectiveness has been
expressed, at the most, in formulating criminal charges
in the trials held by the winners against the losers.
War, the inhuman alternative between killing and
dying, can never be humanized.
War creates inhumanity even when it is not underway,
but is merely a potential threat.
Having this possibility in sight means getting ready for
a competition without measures and without limits.
The possibility of actual warfare coincides with the
certainty of a continuous preparation for it.
There's a logic and a coherence in the unbridled growth
of military expenditures. The "arms race" isn't a trend
limited to a single historical period. If war is a
possibility, the continuous increase of armament
becomes a necessity. The competition for victory is a
conflict that in itself leads to millions of victims. The
result of the unconstrained technological-military
development of a part of the world is the

underdevelopment of another part of it.
Armament costs for 2004 equaled the means available
to live (or not live) of one third of the world's
population.
Abolishing war? A utopia? Yes, of course, if we call
"utopia" what is yet to be, but which instead can and
must be.
Howard Zinn reports in A People's History of the
United States *these astonishing words: "I will say,*
then, that I am not, nor ever have been, in favor of
bringing about in any way the social and political
equality of the white and black races, that I am not,
nor ever have been, in favor of making voters or jurors
of negroes, nor of qualifying them to hold office, nor to
intermarry with white people. And inasmuch they
cannot so live, while they do remain together there
must be the position of superior and inferior, and I as
much as any other man am in favor of having the
superior position assigned to the white race."
This was not expressed during a Ku Klux Klan
gathering, but rather these are the words of Abraham
Lincoln, who in this way intended to draw the line
between what he considered reasonable and what he

thought was "obviously" excluded from any sensible future perspective.

The President, who, five years later, with his Emancipation Proclamation declared all slaves free, expressed his own "realistic view" at a moment when he was trying to win over voters.

During those same years, there were utopians who preached an "unrealistic" equality of rights.

At the beginning of his teaching career, Zinn himself was fired in 1963 from Spelman College in Atlanta, Georgia, for having taken part in the Civil Rights Movement. In 2005, that same college acknowledged his contribution "to knocking down racial barriers."

In forty-two years, the unthinkable, the unacceptable has turned into something unquestionably obvious. Utopia can move at a surprisingly fast pace.

"Abolishing war," eliminating it from the national and international laws seems to be an impossible utopia: it is, instead, an unquestionable and urgent necessity, a goal to be achieved to ensure a future to humanity.

Baghdad, Iraq, June 2003

Just War
Howard Zinn

Thank you for inviting me to Italy. And special thanks to Dr. Gino Strada and Rossella Miccio for arranging this trip, and to them and the whole staff of EMER-GENCY for the magnificent work they are doing to bring a bit of sanity into the madness of war.

I come from a country that is at war, as it has been almost continuously since the end of World War II. The United States has not been invaded for almost two hundred years, not since the year 1812, but it has invaded other countries, again and again, as it is doing at the present, in Iraq, and for that I feel shame. The world has been at war, again and again all through the twentieth century, and here it is, a new century, and we still have not done away with the horror of war. For that we should all feel ashamed.

That shame should not immobilize us. It should provoke us to action.

I want to talk tonight about the persistence of war, and suggest what it is that we might be able to do. Of course we can try to help the victims of war, as EMER-GENCY has done, so heroically. It has cared for a million patients in the last ten years, saving the lives of countless children. But, as Gino Strada writes in the final pages of his book *Green Parrots*, our mission must go beyond helping the victims of war, to abolishing war itself. He asks the question: "Is it monstrous to think about how to create the possibility of human relationships based on equality, on social justice, and on solidarity, and relationships from which the use of violence, terrorism, and war is excluded by common accord?"

So let us think together about that possibility.

We must recognize that we cannot depend on the governments of the world to abolish war because they and the economic interests they represent benefit from war. Therefore, we, the people of the world, must take up the challenge. And although we do not command armies, we do not have great treasuries of wealth, there is one crucial fact that gives us enormous power: the governments of the world cannot wage war without the participation of the people. Albert Einstein understood this simple fact. Horrified by the carnage of World War I in which ten million died in the battlefields of Europe, Einstein said: "Wars will stop when men refuse to fight."

That is our challenge, to bring the world to the point where men will refuse to fight, and governments will be helpless to wage war.

Is that Utopian? Impossible? Only a dream?

Do men go to war because it is part of human nature? If so, then we might consider it impossible to do away with war. But there is no evidence, in biology, or psychology, or anthropology, of a natural instinct for war. If that were so, we would find a spontaneous rush to war by masses of people. What we find is something very different: we find that governments must make enormous efforts to mobilize populations for war. They must entice soldiers with promises of money, land, education, skills. And if those enticements don't work, governments must coerce. They must conscript young people, force them into military service, threaten them with prison of they do not comply.

But the most powerful weapon of governments in raising armies is the weapon of propaganda, of ideology. They must persuade young people, and their families that though they may die, though they may lose arms or legs, or become blind, that it is done for the common good, for a noble cause, for democracy, for liberty, for God, for the country.

The Crusaders of the Middle Ages fought for Christ. The Nazi storm troopers had on their belts "Gott Mit Uns" (God is with us). Young Americans today, asked why they are willing to go to Iraq, will answer: "I owe something to my country." God, liberty, democracy, country—these are all examples of what that great novelist Kurt Vonnegut called "granfaloons"—abstractions, meaningless collections that say nothing about human beings.

The idea that we owe something to our country goes far back, to Plato, who puts into the mouth of Socrates the idea that the citizen has an obligation to

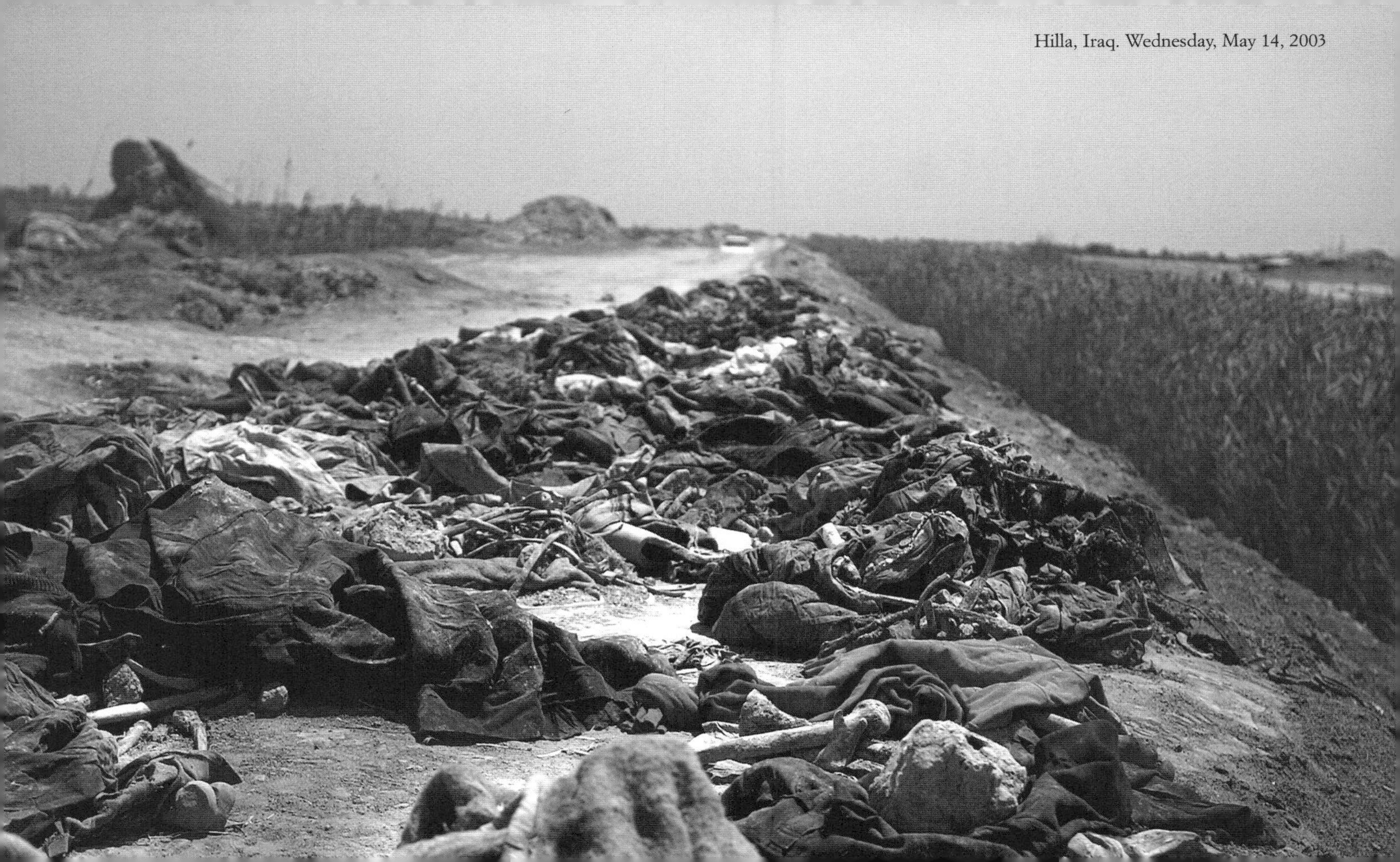

Hilla, Iraq. Wednesday, May 14, 2003

the state, that the state is to be revered more than your father and mother. He says: "In war, and in the court of justice, and everywhere, you must do whatever your state and your country tell you to do, or you must persuade them that their commands are unjust." There is no equality here: the citizen may use persuasion, no more. The state may use force.

This idea of obedience to the state is the essence of totalitarianism. And we find it not only in Mussolini's Italy, in Hitler's Germany, in Stalin's Soviet Union, but in so-called democratic countries, like the United States.

In the United States, every year at the end of May, we celebrate "Memorial Day," which is dedicated to the memory of all those who have died in the nation's wars.

It is a day when bugles blow, and flags are unfurled, and you hear politicians and editorial writers say, again and again: "They gave their lives for their country."

There is a double lie in that short sentence. First, those who died in war did not give their lives—their lives were taken from them by the politicians who sent them to war, politicians who now bow their heads on Memorial Day.

Second, they did not give their lives for "their country" but for the government—in the present instance for Bush and Cheney and Rumsfeld and the corporate executives of Halliburton and Bechtel—all of whom are profiting, either financially or politically, from the military action that has killed over 1,700 Americans and countless Iraqis. No, they did not die for their country. The ordinary people who make up the country get no benefits from the blood shed in Iraq.

When the United States was born, in revolt against British rule, it adopted a Declaration of Independence, which states the fundamental principle of a democracy, that there is a difference between the country, the people, on one side, and the government on the other side. The government is an artificial creation, established by the people to defend everyone's equal right to life, liberty, and the pursuit of happiness. And when the government does not fulfill that obligation, it is the right of the people, in the words of the Declaration of Independence, to "alter or abolish" the government.

In other words, when government acts against life, liberty, the pursuit of happiness, disobedience to government is a necessary principle of democracy. If we care about democracy, we must remind young people of that principle, especially when they are asked to go to war.

It is a tribute to the natural instincts of people, to preserve life, to care for other people, that governments must use all the powers at their command—bribery, coercion, propaganda—to overcome those natural instincts and persuade a nation that it must go to war.

When the United States government decided, in

1917, to join the slaughter that was taking place in Europe, it did not find a population eager for war. Indeed, Woodrow Wilson, running for President in 1916, promised that the United States would remain neutral in the war, saying: "There is such a thing as a nation being too proud to fight."

But the economic ties with England, the huge loans of American bankers to England that would be jeopardized by defeat in war, pushed Wilson, after he was elected, to ask Congress to declare war on Germany.

The American people did not rush to support the war. A million men were needed, but in the first six weeks after the declaration of war by Congress only 73,000 volunteered. And so the government turned to coercion. It instituted conscription, and now young men would be compelled, by the threat of imprisonment, to join the military.

But coercion would not be effective if the nation could not be convinced that this was a just war, a war, as President Wilson said, "to end all wars," a war "to make the world safe for democracy." And so the government launched the most massive propaganda campaign in history to persuade the American people that the war in Europe was worth fighting, even if it meant sacrificing the lives of their sons, their brothers, their husbands. A committee on Public Information was established, which sponsored 75,000 speakers who roamed the country, giving 750,000 speeches in 5,000 American cities and towns.

Opposition to the war was widespread. The Socialist Party, which at that time, was a major force in American life, immediately called the declaration of war "a crime against the people of the United States." There were anti-war rallies all over the country, and acts of resistance against the draft. In New York City, of the first hundred men drafted for military service, ninety claimed exemption. In Florida, two Negro farm hands went into the woods with a shotgun and mutilated themselves to avoid the draft. Hundreds of thousands of men evaded the draft.

The government used all its powers to suppress opposition. It passed an Espionage Act which made it a crime to discourage enlistment in the armed forces. Two thousand people were prosecuted under this act, and a thousand sent to prison, including the leader of the Socialist Party, Eugene Debs.

But when the war ended in 1918, the horror of it all slowly came into the consciousness of people all over the world. Ten million men had died on the battlefields of Europe. In one battle early in the war, there were 500,000 casualties on each side. In the first three months of the war, almost the entire original British army was wiped out. Battles were fought over a few hundred yards of earth, leaving the land strewn with corpses.

After the war, with twenty million wounded, with the war veterans visible everywhere, shell-shocked, without arms or legs, blinded, the full picture of the

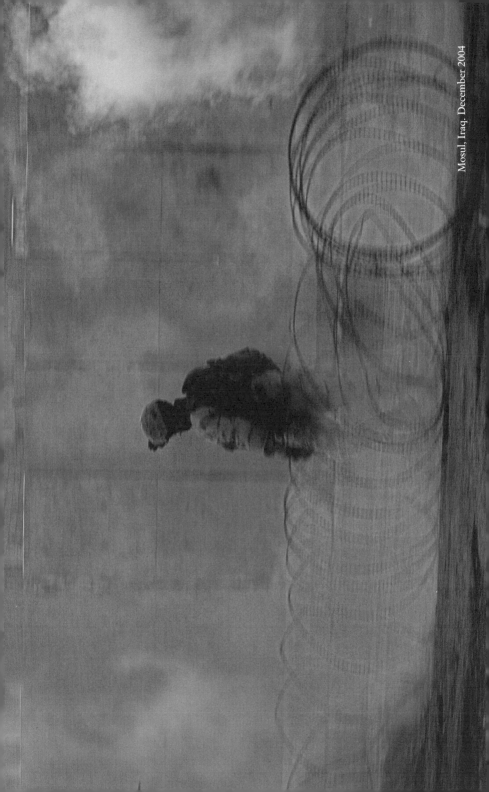

Mosul, Iraq. December 2004

war began to be known. A literature of disillusionment appeared. Erich Maria Remarque wrote that while men by the thousands were being blown apart by machine guns and shells, the official dispatches were telling the German people back home, "All Quiet on the Western Front." The bitter war poems of Wilfred Owen, who fought and died in the British army, were published and Ernest Hemingway wrote *A Farewell to Arms*.

The idea of a just war, a good war, a war for democracy, for liberty, a war to end all wars seemed, in 1918, to be thoroughly discredited. War had been revealed in all its ugliness and no one could point to any good that had come out of the sacrifice of all those human beings.

All over the world, more and more people recognized that the Great War of 1914–1918, which had pretended to be a war against the tyranny of the German Kaiser, a war, as Wilson had put it "to make the world safe for democracy," had in reality been a struggle among imperial powers, at the cost of millions of young lives. Indeed, the general revulsion against war was great enough to cause sixty-two nations to sign the Kellogg-Briand Pact, which declared that war could not be accepted as "an instrument of national policy."

But already Fascism was on the march in Europe. The first sign of its aggressiveness towards other countries came with the Italian bombardment and conquest of Ethiopia in 1935. Hitler was now in power in Germany, and soon he had taken over Austria. Hitler and Mussolini together enabled Franco to take power in Spain, then the Nazis marched into Czechoslovakia in 1938, invaded Poland in September 1939, and World War II had begun.

Now the idea of the just war, the good war, received its most powerful support.

What could be more justifiable than a war against Fascism, which was ruthlessly crushing dissent at home, and taking over other countries, while proclaiming theories of racial supremacy and promoting a spirit of nationalist arrogance. When Japan, which was committing atrocities in China, allied itself to Italy and Germany, and then attacked the U.S. fleet at Pearl Harbor, it seemed to be clear—it was the democratic countries against the Fascist countries.

Let me tell you a little about myself, because I grew up in the thirties and I want to tell you how my own thinking about war changed over the years. As a young boy growing up in the United States, I read adventure novels about World War I that presented it as a story of military heroism and comradeship. It was war, clean and glorious, without death or suffering.

That romantic view of war was totally extinguished when, at the age of eighteen, I read a book by a Hollywood screenwriter named Dalton Trumbo. In later years, he would be imprisoned for refusing to talk to a Congressional committee about his political affiliations. Trumbo's book was called *Johnny Got His Gun*. Written some years after World War I, it is, perhaps, the most disturbing anti-war novel ever written.

Here was war in its ultimate horror. On one of the battlefields of World War I they had found a slab of flesh in an American uniform, with no legs, no arms, no face, blind, deaf, unable to speak, but still alive, the heart still beating, the brain still functioning, able to think about his past, ponder his present condition, and wonder if he will ever be able to communicate with the world outside. For him, the oratory of the politicians who sent him off to war—the language of freedom, democracy, and patriotism—is now seen as the ultimate hypocrisy.

He is a mute, thinking torso on a hospital bed, but he finds a way to communicate with a kindly nurse, and when a visiting delegation of military officials comes by to pin a medal on his body, he taps out a message. He says: "Take me into the workplaces, into the schools, show me to the little children and to the college students, let them see what war is like. Take me wherever there are parliaments and diets and congresses and chambers of statesmen. I want to be there when they talk about honor and justice and making the world safe for democracy . . . But before they give the order for all the little guys to start killing each other let the main guy rap his gavel on my case and point down at me and say here gentlemen is the only issue before this house and that is are you for this thing here or are you against it."

That novel, *Johnny Got His Gun*, had a shattering effect on me when I read it. It left me with a bone-deep hatred of war. This was reinforced by a class-consciousness, which came from my growing up in a poor working class family. I agreed with the judgment of the Roman biographer Plutarch, who said: "The poor go to war, to fight and die for the delights, riches, and superfluities of others." I agreed with the Socialist leader Eugene Debs, who told a crowd of Americans in 1917: "Wars throughout history have been waged for conquest and plunder . . . The master class has always declared the wars; the subject class has always fought the battles."

And yet, in early 1943, at the age of twenty, I volunteered for the Army Air Force.

Bombing raids were going on every day and night over Europe. I wanted to make my contribution to the defeat of Fascism. Yes, I had learned to hate war, but this war, I thought, was not for profit or empire, it was a people's war, a war against the unspeakable brutality of Fascism.

I had been reading about Italian Fascism in a book about Mussolini, by journalist George Seldes, called *Sawdust Caesar*. I was inspired by his account of the Socialist Matteotti, who stood in the Italian Chamber of Deputies to denounce the establishment of a dictatorship. The black-shirted thugs of Mussolini's party picked up Matteotti outside his home one morning and shot him to death. That was Fascism.

Mussolini's Italy, deciding to restore the glory of the old Roman Empire, invaded the East African coun-

Nepalgunj, Nepal. June 2005

try of Ethiopia, a pitifully poor country. Its people, armed with spears and muskets, tried to fight off an Italian army equipped with the most modern weapons and with an air force that, unopposed, dropped bombs on Ethiopian towns and villages. It was a slaughter. The American black poet Langston Hughes wrote, in bitterness: "The little fox is still / The dogs of war have made their kill."

I was thirteen when this happened and was only vaguely aware of headlines: "Italian Planes Bomb Addis Ababa." But I later read about this and about the rise of Hitler, the attacks on the Jews, the beatings and murders of opponents, the shrill oratory of the little man with the mustache, the monster rallies of hysterical Germans shouting "Heil Hitler!"

I became part of a crew on a B-17, a heavy bomber that flew out of England over the continent. I dropped bombs on Berlin, on other cities in Germany, Hungary, Czechoslovakia, and even on a small town on the Atlantic coast of France. I never questioned anything I did. Fascism had to be resisted and defeated. I flew the last bombing missions of the war, received my Air Medal and my battle stars, and was quietly proud of my participation in the great war to defeat Fascism. I had no doubts. This was a just war.

And yet, when I packed up my things at the end of the war and put my old navigation logs and snapshots and other mementos in a folder, I marked that folder, almost without thinking, "Never Again."

I'm still not sure why I did that, but I suppose I was beginning, unconsciously, to do what I would later do consciously: to question the motives, the conduct, and the consequences of that crusade against Fascism. It was not that my abhorrence of Fascism was in any way diminished. But that clear certainty of moral rightness that propelled me into the Air Force as an enthusiastic bombardier was now clouded over by many thoughts.

Perhaps the doubts started in the midst of my bombing missions in my conversations with a gunner on another crew. To my astonishment he spoke of the war as an "imperialist war," fought on both sides for national power. Britain and the United States were opposing Fascism only because it threatened their own control over resources and people.

Yes, Hitler was a maniacal dictator and invader of other countries. But what of the British Empire and its long history of wars against native peoples to subdue them for the profit and glory of the empire? And the Soviet Union—was it not also a brutal dictatorship, concerned not with the working classes of the world but with its own national power? And what of my own country, with its imperial ambitions in Latin America and Asia? The United States had entered the war not when the Japanese were committing atrocities against China, but only when Japan attacked Pearl Harbor in Hawaii, a colony of the United States.

These were troubling questions, but I continued

to fly my bombing missions. Ironically, my radical friend, who called it an imperialist war, was killed in a mission over Germany not long after our conversation.

When the war in Europe ended, my crew flew back to the United States in the same plane we were in for our bombing missions. We were given a thirty-day leave and then were supposed to go to the Pacific to fly bombing missions against the Japanese. My wife and I had been married before I went overseas. We decided to spend some time in the countryside before I had to go to the Pacific. On the way to the bus station we passed a newsstand. It was August 7, 1945. There was a huge headline: "Atomic Bomb Dropped on Hiroshima, City Destroyed." I had no idea what an atomic bomb was, but I remember my feeling at the time, a sense of relief: the war would be over soon, I would not have to go to the Pacific.

Shortly after the war ended, something important happened to cause me to think differently about Hiroshima and also to rethink my belief that we had been engaged in a "just war." I read the report of a journalist, John Hersey, who went into Hiroshima shortly after the bombing and talked to survivors. You can imagine what those survivors looked like—some without arms, others without legs, others blinded or with their skin so burned that you could not look at them. I read their stories, and for the first time I realized the human consequences of bombing.

For the first time it came to me that I had no idea

what I was doing to human beings when I was dropping bombs on cities in Europe. When you drop bombs from six miles (perhaps eight kilometers) in the sky, you do not see what is happening down below. You do not hear screams, or see blood. You do not see children torn apart in the explosions of your bombs. I began to understand how in times of war atrocities are committed by ordinary people, who do not see their victims up close as human beings, who only see them as "the enemy," though they may be five years old.

I thought now about a bombing raid I had flown just weeks before the end of the war. Near a little town on the Atlantic coast of France, called Royan, there was an encampment of German soldiers. They were not doing anything, just waiting for the war to end. Our crew and a thousand other crews were ordered to drop bombs on the area of Royan, and were told we would be using a new type of bomb called jellied gasoline. It was napalm. Several thousand people were killed, German soldiers, French civilians, but flying at high altitude I saw no human beings, no children burned by napalm. The town of Royan was destroyed.

I did not think about that until I read later about the victims of Hiroshima and Nagasaki. I visited Royan twenty years after the war, did some research, and realized that people had died because someone wanted more medals, and someone on high wanted to test what napalm would do to human flesh.

I then began to think about the Allied bombing of

Mosul, Iraq. December 2004

civilian populations all through the war. We had been horrified when the Italians bombed Addis Ababa, when the Germans bombed Coventry and London and Rotterdam. But when the Allied leaders met at Casablanca in early 1943 they agreed on massive air attacks to undermine the morale of the German people. Winston Churchill and his advisors, with the knowledge of the American high command, decided that bombing the working-class districts of Germany would accomplish that.

And so the saturation bombing began, of Frankfurt, Cologne, Hamburg, killing tens of thousands in each city. It was terror bombing. And in February 1945, the German city of Dresden was attacked in one day and one night of bombing by British and American planes, and when the intense heat generated by the bombs created a vacuum, a gigantic fire storm swept the city, which was full of refugees at the time. Perhaps fifty thousand or a hundred thousand people were killed. No one knows exactly how many.

I studied the circumstances of the bombing of Hiroshima and Nagasaki, and concluded, as did the most serious scholars of those incidents, that all the excuses given for those horrors were false. Those bombings were not necessary to bring the war to an end because the Japanese were on the verge of surrender. One motivation for them was political—they were the first acts of the cold war between the United States and the Soviet Union, with several hundred thousand innocent Japanese people as guinea pigs. Even before the atomic bombing, in the spring of 1945, there was a night attack on Tokyo that set the city afire. There was no pretense of precision bombing, and perhaps a hundred thousand men, women, children died.

I gradually came to certain conclusions about war, any war, even a so-called "good war," a "just war" to defeat Fascism. I decided that war corrupts everyone who engages in it, that it poisons the minds and souls of people on all sides. I realized there was a process by which I and others had become unthinking killers of innocent people. A decision is made at the start of a war that your side is good and the other side is bad, and once you make that decision you don't have to think any more; anything you do, no matter how horrible, is acceptable.

I also realized that the idea of just war is based on several logical fallacies. One of them is that if the other side is evil—as Fascism certainly was—then it means that your side must be good. Another fallacy involves a jump in logic that happens unconsciously, but which should be examined. The jump is this: that a cause may indeed be just—a country has been invaded, a tyrant is in power, something wrong has taken place—but then the reality of a just cause blends almost imperceptibly into the idea of a just war. In other words, a cause may be just, an injustice may have taken place, but that doesn't mean that the use of war to remedy that injustice is itself just. It is time to consider an idea that is not part of conventional thinking about international relations—that if there are injustices in the world, whatever they are, we must search for a way to remedy them without war.

We must recognize something else. That in going to war against a nation which is ruled by a tyrant, the people you kill are the victims of the tyrant. Gino Strada points out in his book that as wars have developed in the twentieth century, the ratio of civilian deaths to military deaths has changed radically. In World War I, there were ten times as many deaths of soldiers as civilians. By the time of World War II, 65% of the dead were civilians.

And when we come to our time, the wars in Vietnam, Afghanistan, Iraq, 90% of the victims are civilians. In Afghanistan, Dr. Strada, studying 4,000 patients who were operated on, found that 93% were civilians, and 34% were children less than fourteen years of age. In the other war zones he has been in, he found it was no different.

War, we must realize, is the massive and indiscriminate killing of human beings. War is always fundamentally a war against children. And therefore, whatever just cause is presented to us, whether true or invented, whatever words are thrown at us about fighting for liberty or democracy or against tyranny, we must reject war as a solution. In 1932, Albert Einstein was in Geneva, where delegates from sixty nations had gathered to draw up rules for the conduct of war. Einstein was horrified. He did something he had never done, called a press conference, and said the gathering was mistaken. War, he said, cannot be humanized. It can only be abolished.

The idea of a just war begins to disintegrate when you extend your time frame beyond the immediate consequences of the war—which may seem a great victory for humanity over evil—and look at the long term consequences. In World War II, which is the model for the idea of a just war, there was great joy over the defeat of Germany, Italy, Japan. I remember vividly May 8, 1945, the day called V-E Day, Victory in Europe, when our air crew drove to the town of Norwich in England, and the city, which had been dark for five years in fear of air raids, was ablaze with light and everyone was out in the street, singing and shouting for joy.

Yes, we were right to celebrate. Hitler was dead, the Japanese military machine was destroyed, Mussolini was hanging in a town square. But, looking at the world after the war, was Fascism really defeated? The elements of Fascism—totalitarianism, racism—were still alive all over the world? Was militarism defeated? No, there were now two superpowers, armed with thousands of nuclear weapons, which if used would make Hitler's holocaust look insignificant. And after fifty million died in World War II, was this the end of war? No, wars continued over the next decades, and tens of millions of people died in these wars.

Pec, Kosovo. June 1999

Mitrovica. Kosovo. July 1999

When I was discharged from the Air Force, I received a letter from General George Marshall, commander of all the armed forces, congratulating me and the sixteen million other Americans who had served in the military and telling me it would now be a different world. But as the years went by it became more and more clear that it was not a different world. I came to the conclusion that war, even a victorious war over an evil enemy, as in the war against Fascism, is a quick fix, like a drug, which gives you a rush of euphoria, but when it wears away you are back in the depths and you must have another fix, another war. Yes, war is an addiction that we must decide to break, for the sake of the children of the world.

I want to point to a characteristic which is true of all wars, even so-called "just" wars, like World War II, or "humanitarian" wars, as some people described the bombing campaign in 1999 in Kosovo and Yugoslavia. We need to think about the moral equation of means and ends. Both Catholic theologians and moral philosophers talk about "proportionality." They argue that if the end, the goal, is important enough, then it is morally acceptable to use war as a means of achieving that end. But I believe we have reached the point in human history where the technology of war has become so horrendous—the cluster bombs, the napalm, the land-mines—that no conceivable end can justify their use. Furthermore, when you go to war, there is certainty about the awfulness of the means, but always uncertainty about what will be the result, what will be the end.

I have spent some time talking about World War II because it is the classic example of the just war, the good war, the humanitarian war. I insist on talking about it also because its immoral elements have not been examined. And if, on examination, we find disturbing questions about this best of wars, this most humanitarian of wars, then what can we say to justify any other war? There was a moral core to World War II that makes the issue of a just war complicated. But where is the moral core in any of the wars fought in the second-half of this century? They have shed the blood of millions of human beings, have mutilated the bodies of old people and children, have driven millions of people out of their homes, have left a hundred million land-mines buried around the world, killing thousands more every year.

Examine the wars fought by my government, the United States. In Korea, three million people dead, after ferocious bombing and the use of napalm. In Vietnam, Cambodia, and Laos, another three million dead. The idea of just war, discredited by World War I, had been revived by World War II. But the experience of the Vietnam War once again gave war a bad name, as more and more Americans realized they had been deceived by the government and decided they could not justify a war that killed 58,000 Americans and millions of Vietnamese.

After Vietnam, the U.S. government tried desperately to eliminate what was called "the Vietnam syndrome." The word "syndrome" suggests a disease. And the disease was the American people's loss of faith in the government and the unwillingness of the citizenry to support a war. The United States decided it must make war acceptable once more, and it would do this by fighting wars only against weak opponents, where the wars would end quickly, with few U.S. casualties, and without giving enough time for an anti-war movement to develop. Also, the government decided it must control the public's information more tightly, to be able to persuade the citizens of the necessity for war.

You can see this strategy at work in Ronald Reagan's administration, with the ridiculous attack on the tiny island of Grenada, in the Caribbean Sea. You can see it in George Bush, Sr.'s invasion of Panama in 1989, which destroyed entire neighborhoods, killed hundreds, perhaps thousands of people. You can see it in the first Gulf War against Iraq in 1991. Where was there even an ounce of justice in these wars? Lies were told to the American public to justify them. But they were soon discredited: was tiny Grenada a threat to the United States? Did we invade Panama to stop the traffic in drugs—the drug trade is flourishing there more than ever? Did we invade Iraq because George Bush, Sr. was heartbroken about the Iraqi invasion of Kuwait? That is hard to believe. Oil seems a much more plausible reason.

In all of these cases: few American casualties, information strictly controlled, and large numbers of Iraqi civilians killed. When General Colin Powell, at the end of the first Iraq war, boasted about the quick victory and only a few hundred U.S. casualties, he was asked about Iraqi casualties and he responded: "That is not a matter I am terribly concerned with."

The new Bush administration came into office under a cloud. Though he received less votes than his opponent, Bush was made President only because a 5-4 vote of the Supreme Court refused to allow a recount of the votes in the state of Florida. He desperately needed to give his presidency some credibility. And he knew that historically, whenever the nation went to war, the people immediately rallied to the support of the President. Add to these motives what was at the heart of U.S. policy in the Middle East ever since the end of World War II—the desire to control the oil resources of that region.

The events of September 11, 2001, the destruction of the Twin Towers in New York and the deaths of 3000 people, gave the Bush administration what it needed, a justification for going to war. Bush announced a "war on terrorism," and immediately ordered the bombing and invasion of Afghanistan. The justification was that Afghanistan was harboring Osama Bin Laden, who was considered responsible for the attacks of 9-11. It was not known exactly where Osama Bin Laden was hiding. But the entire country of

Tawangh, Rolpa District, Nepal, June 2005

Kathmandu, Nepal, June 2005

Afghanistan was now a target. It was a strange way of thinking. If a criminal is hiding in a neighborhood and you don't know in which house he is hiding, you destroy the whole neighborhood.

What could be more just than a war on terrorism? The horrors of 9-ll created an atmosphere of fear in the United States. This was magnified by the government and the media into a kind of hysteria that prevented people from realizing that a war on terrorism contains an internal contradiction, because war itself is terrorism. Indeed, war is the extreme form of terrorism. No group of terrorists anywhere in the world can match the capacity for mass murder possessed by nations.

Every day during the bombing of Afghanistan, *The New York Times* showed the photos and biographies of victims of the 9-11 attacks. It was an important thing to do, to see the victims as human beings. But the press did nothing like that for the Afghan people who were dying in the war. The control of information by the government, with the cooperation of the media, allowed the United States to present the war as a just war, a war against terrorism and thus gain popular support. It was a short war, with few U.S. casualties, with the public kept ignorant of the fact that more Afghans had died in the U.S. bombing campaign than were killed in the Twin Towers, that hundreds of thousands had been terrorized, driven from their homes.

The success of the U.S. government in getting public support for the war in Afghanistan encouraged it to do what we now know, from the testimony of officials close to the White House, what it wanted to do even before the attacks of 9-11: to invade Iraq.

And so it set out to persuade the public that Iraq was a danger to the world, that it had weapons of mass destruction. The major newspapers and television networks dutifully reported, without criticism, what the government was saying. When Colin Powell appeared before the United Nations and presented a detailed list, which turned out to be completely false, of Iraq's weapons, *The New York Times*, considered the nation's leading liberal newspaper, praised his presentation.

The United Nations refused to go along with the plans for war on Iraq, but the United States prepared for war. On Feb 15, 2003 something happened that had never happened before in human history: simultaneously, on that one day, ten to fifteen million people all over the world protested against the war. In the United States, hundreds of thousands of people, in towns and cities all over the country, demonstrated against the coming war. The day after that world-wide protest, a *New York Times* reporter wrote: "There are now two superpowers—the United States, and world public opinion."

A ferocious bombing of Iraq began. The phrase "shock and awe" was used proudly by the officials of the U.S. government as thousands of innocent Iraqis were dying in the attack and hundreds of thousands fled the cities to become homeless refugees. The U.S.

army entered Baghdad and President Bush proudly proclaimed: "Mission Accomplished." But, as we know, the war did not end with the taking of Baghdad, or even with the capture of Saddam Hussein. It is still going on, two years later. The major media have been reluctant to criticize the war and the Bush Administration. When Bush earlier this year delivered his Inaugural Address, *The New York Times* gave it a huge headline, "BUSH, AT 2ND INAUGURAL, SAYS SPREAD OF LIBERTY IS THE CALLING OF OUR TIME." The *Times*' editorial admired his speech.

Despite this, the truth about the war has been coming through to the American public even in the major media. Every day there is a report of one or two or six U.S. military who were killed in Iraq. And though the Bush Administration, with the cooperation of the press, has not publicized the ten thousand or more Americans who have been wounded in the war— some blinded, some with legs or arms amputated—the information is beginning to come through. Whatever idea there was in the minds of many Americans that this was a "just war" has begun to fall apart.

The American public has been mostly kept ignorant of what this war has done to the Iraqi people— very few know that a prestigious international team of researchers has concluded that anywhere from 25,000 to 100,000 Iraqis have died in this war. Occasionally, a glimpse of the horror comes through even in the media. Two days before Bush's Inaugural speech, there was, on an inside page of *The New York Times*, a photo of a little girl, crouching, covered with blood, weeping. The caption read: "An Iraqi girl screamed yesterday after her parents were killed when American soldiers fired on their car when it failed to stop, despite warning shots . . ."

More and more, the lies of the Bush Administration have been exposed—the lies about weapons of mass destruction, the lies about Iraq's connection to Al Qaida, the covering up of the Bush's secret plans, even before 9-11, for the invasion of Iraq. More and more Americans have become aware that Iraq has been invaded, not just by soldiers, but by American corporations, by Halliburton and Bechtel, who have been awarded billions of dollars in contracts to support the occupation. Americans are much more class-conscious than is realized by people in other parts of the world. They understand that our society is dominated by the wealthy classes, and that wars bring huge profits to some. During the Vietnam War, one of the most effective posters of the anti-war movement, made by a well-known artist, said, simply, chillingly: "War is good for business. Invest your son."

There has been a slow seeping of information to the public, some of it even through the major media, much of it through alternative literature: books, progressive radio programs, documentary films (Michael Moore's pre-election film was seen by millions). The Internet has been an important source of information

Gardez, Afghanistan. May 2005

Kfar Darom Settlement, Gaza, Palestine. Thursday, August 18, 2005

not available in the mainstream media, and also a useful organizing tool, making it possible for groups around the country to communicate with one another instantly. Let us go back to Einstein who said: "Wars will stop when men refuse to fight." This is beginning to happen in Iraq. Thousands of soldiers have deserted. Some have spoken out publicly against the war. The Pentagon reports that it has trouble recruiting new soldiers. Families of people in the military—some of them have lost sons or daughters—are criticizing the war. In March, marking two years of war, there were anti-war protests in 800 communities across the United States. In one small city, Fayetteville, North Carolina, near an important military base, there was a demonstration of thousands, listening to veterans from Iraq and a mother whose son was killed—all of them calling for an end to the war.

According to the latest public opinion surveys, Bush no longer has majority approval for his policies. Two years ago, only 20% of the public disapproved of the war in Iraq. As of last week, 60% of those polled said they did not believe in the war.

We have learned from historical experience that people can change their opinions dramatically if they get new information. At the start of the war in Vietnam, 60% of the American people supported the war. A few years later, 60% opposed the war. The reason for that turnaround in public opinion is that the truth about the war gradually emerged. The numbers of dead and wounded kept growing. And people slowly became aware that atrocities were being committed in Vietnam, that U.S. bombers were destroying peasant villages. Photos appeared of the My Lai Massacre, when U.S. soldiers executed 400 to 500 peasants, mostly old people, women, and children, in a small village. There was a photo of a young Vietnamese girl running along a road, her skin burned and shredding, from napalm.

That suggests to us what we must do if we are to rid the world of war, not just this particular war, but war in general. We need, all of us, to become teachers, to spread information. We need to expose the motives of our political leaders, point out their connections to corporate power, show how huge profits are being made out of death and suffering.

We need to teach history, because when you look at the history of wars, you see how war corrupts everyone involved in it, how the so-called good side soon behaves like the bad side, how this has been true from the Peloponnesian War all the way to our own time.

And most important, we have to show, in the most graphic way, as Gino Strada has done in his book *Green Parrots*, the effect of war on human beings. And how wars, even when they are over, leave a legacy of death in the form of land-mines, and a legacy of mental disturbance in the soldiers who return from war.

We need to point to the reckless waste of the world's wealth in war and militarism, while a billion people in the world are without clean water, and a hundred million suffer from AIDS and other deadly illnesses. Dr. Strada reminds us that nine million people die of hunger every year. A fraction of the money spent on war and preparations for war would save the lives of tens of millions of people.

We need to hold out a vision of a different world, in which national borders are erased and we are truly one human family, in which we treat children all over the world as our children, which means we could never engage in war.

The abolition of war is of course an enormous undertaking. But keep in mind that we in the anti-war movement have a powerful ally. Our ally is a truth that even governments addicted to war, profiting from war, must one of these days recognize: that wars are not practical ways of achieving their ends. More and more, in recent history, the most powerful nations find themselves unable to conquer much weaker nations. The United States, with the most deadly military machine in the world, could not win in Korea. It could not win in Vietnam. The Soviet Union, with all its power, was forced finally to withdraw from Afghanistan. And the American victory in Afghanistan has turned out to be a sham, as the warlords are back in power in most of the country.

As for Iraq, we can see what is happening. What looked like a victory in Iraq is turning out to be a disaster, as the insurgency against the U.S. occupation not only continues, but grows. There was an embarrassing moment last week when reporters pressed the White House press secretary about Vice-President Cheney's recent remark that the insurgency was "in its last throes." "Where is the evidence for that?" he was asked. He stumbled and stumbled and could not answer the question.

Perhaps it will take a combination of factors to end war. It will become intolerable for the people and impractical for the Establishment. And the crucial factor making it impractical will be, as it was for the Soviet Union in Afghanistan and the United States in Vietnam, that the citizens of war-making nations will no longer tolerate the deaths of their offspring and the theft of their national wealth.

There is still time to make this twenty-first century different from the last century. But we must all play a part.

Auschwitz, Poland. December 2003

Appendix

Howard Zinn

Howard Zinn—historian, playwright and social activist—is one of our most celebrated contemporary minds. He has taught at Spelman College in Atlanta, at Boston University, and has been a visiting professor at the University of Paris and the University of Bologna. He was active in the Civil Rights Movement, and has always been a dedicated critical voice against the horrors of war and the quiet acceptance of conquest and murder in the name of progress. He received the Thomas Merton Award, the Eugene V. Debs Award, the Upton Sinclair Award and the Lannan Literary Award. He has written many books, his best known being *A People's History of the United States*, which narrates America's history from the point of view of, and in the words of, women, factory workers, minorities, the working poor, and immigrants. He is an active columnist for *The Progressive* and has given innumerable contributions to other publications. His work—a unique integration of clear prose, scholarly research, and inspiring hope for a better future—is well-known outside the United States and belongs to all the progressives of the world. In a world of conflict, victims, and executioners, he has inspired generations of thinking people to have respect and compassion for victims, rather than accepting complacency and inaction.

Gino Strada

Specialized in emergency surgery, during the eighties Gino Strada was mainly involved in transplants, with extended periods of training in the United States and internships both in Great Britain and South Africa.

In 1988, he decided to use his experience to assist and treat victims of armed conflict. Between 1989 and 1992 Strada worked with the International Red Cross of Geneva in various war-torn areas. This convinced him of the necessity to create an organization that could intervene in favor of civilians suffering the consequences of war.

With very few means, in the spring of 1994 he founded in Milan, together with a group of friends and colleagues, EMERGENCY. That same year, in August, he re-opened the hospital of Rwanda's capital, Kigali, which had been abandoned and devastated by war. EMERGENCY, with small but numerous donations from private supporters, built the first hospital in North Iraq (in Sulaimaniya) in 1996, and over the following years the organization worked in other areas devastated by armed conflicts, including Cambodia, Afghanistan, and Sierra Leone.

By December 2004, EMERGENCY had treated well over one million people.

EMERGENCY's efforts against anti-personnel mines have been decisive, paving the way for the law that abolished the production of these devices in Italy (October 1997).

In May 1996, *Scientific American* dedicated its cover to an article, entitled "The Horror of Land Mines," by Dr. Strada. In 1999, *Pappagalli Verdi, cronache di un chirurgo di guerra* (Feltrinelli; English edition: *Green Parrots, A War Surgeon's Diary*, Charta 2004) was published and awarded the Premio Internazionale Viareggio. It was followed in 2002 by *Buskashi, viaggio dentro la guerra* (Feltrinelli).

In November 2004, EMERGENCY announced its project of the *Salam* (Peace) Center for Cardiac Surgery in Khartoum to provide services to patients in Sudan and its surrounding countries.

EMERGENCY USA was founded in February 2005. Strada kicked off the organization's activities in America with a series of talks in many cities across the country to present the organization's work in the world.

Moises Saman

Moises Saman was born in Lima, Peru, in 1974. As a young child his family moved from his father's hometown of Lima to Barcelona, Spain, his mother's home, where he became a Spanish citizen. At the age of eighteen he moved to Los Angeles to study photography at California State University, Fullerton. During his junior year in college, he took his first trip to a conflict zone, traveling to the troubled southern Mexican state of Chiapas, photographing the aftermath of the Zapatista uprising (1995). After graduating he interned at *Newsday* in New York. Shortly thereafter, Saman set out for the war-torn Balkans, where he spent a month traveling through Kosovo during the summer of 1999. Upon returning to New York in 2000, he was hired as a full-time photographer by *Newsday*, where he remains on staff. At *Newsday* he has concentrated on international assignments and has covered immigration stories in Central America, the Israeli-Palestinian conflict, the war in Afghanistan (since September 2001), and most recently, beginning in October 2002, the escalation that led to the war in Iraq. He was one of few photographers working for an American newspaper that remained in Baghdad during the coalition bombing campaign. On March 24, 2003 Saman was arrested, along with four foreign journalists, and accused of espionage by the Iraqi secret police. He spent eight days in prison before he was deported to Jordan. He has since returned to Iraq, Afghanistan, and Palestine on various occasions to continue his coverage of the ongoing conflicts. Saman is currently working on projects in Nepal and Haiti. A selection of his work in Nepal was featured in the November 2005 issue of *Photo District News* (*PDN*). His photographs were featured in a traveling group exhibition entitled *The Art of Aggression* and in the September 2003 and 2005 editions of Visa pour L'Image, the International Photojournalism Festival in Perpignan, France. He was awarded a *Newsday* Publisher's Award twice (in 2001 and 2003). In 2004, he received the second prize in single photographs in the prestigious World Press Photo Award for General News and was a participant in the 2004 World Press Photo Masterclass.

Contents

Design
Gabriele Nason
with Daniela Meda

Editorial Coordination
Filomena Moscatelli

Editing and Translatiom
Emily Ligniti

Copywriting and Press Office
Silvia Palombi Arte&Mostre, Milano

Web Design and On-line Promotion
Barbara Bonacina

© 2005
Edizioni Charta, Milano

© The authors for their texts

For his photographs
Saman © 2005 Newsday, Inc., New
York Reprinted with permission

© Moises Saman for photographs
Pec, Kosovo, June 1999 - p. 40
Mitrovica, Kosovo, July 1999 - p. 41

ISBN 88-8158-572-3

Edizioni Charta
via della Moscova, 27
20121 Milano
Tel. +39-026598098/026598200
Fax +39-026598577
e-mail: edcharta@tin.it
www.chartaartbooks.it

Printed in Italy

To find out more about Charta, and to learn
about our most recent publications, visit

www.chartaartbooks.it

Printed in December 2005
by Leva spa, Sesto San Giovanni
for Edizioni Charta